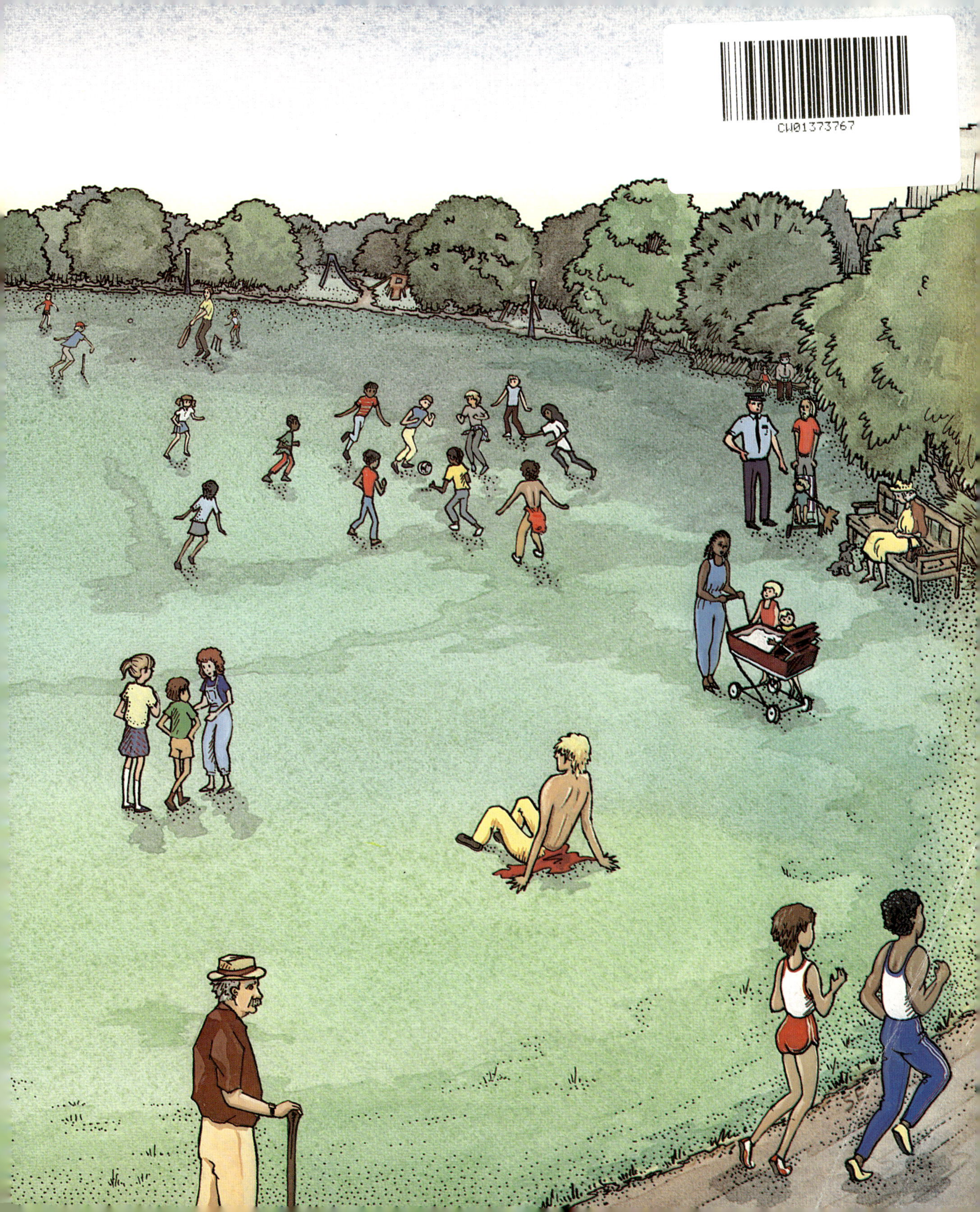

For Dominic

First published 1986
Published by Hamish Hamilton Children's Books
Garden House 57–59 Long Acre London WC2E 9JZ
Text copyright © 1986 by Saviour Pirotta
Illustrations copyright © 1986 by Su Eaton
All Rights Reserved

British Library Cataloguing in Publication Data
Pirotta, Saviour
Let the shadows fly
I. Title
823'.914[J] PZ7
ISBN 0-241-11800-X

Printed in Great Britain by
Cambus Litho, East Kilbride

Let the Shadows Fly

Saviour Pirotta

Illustrated by Su Eaton

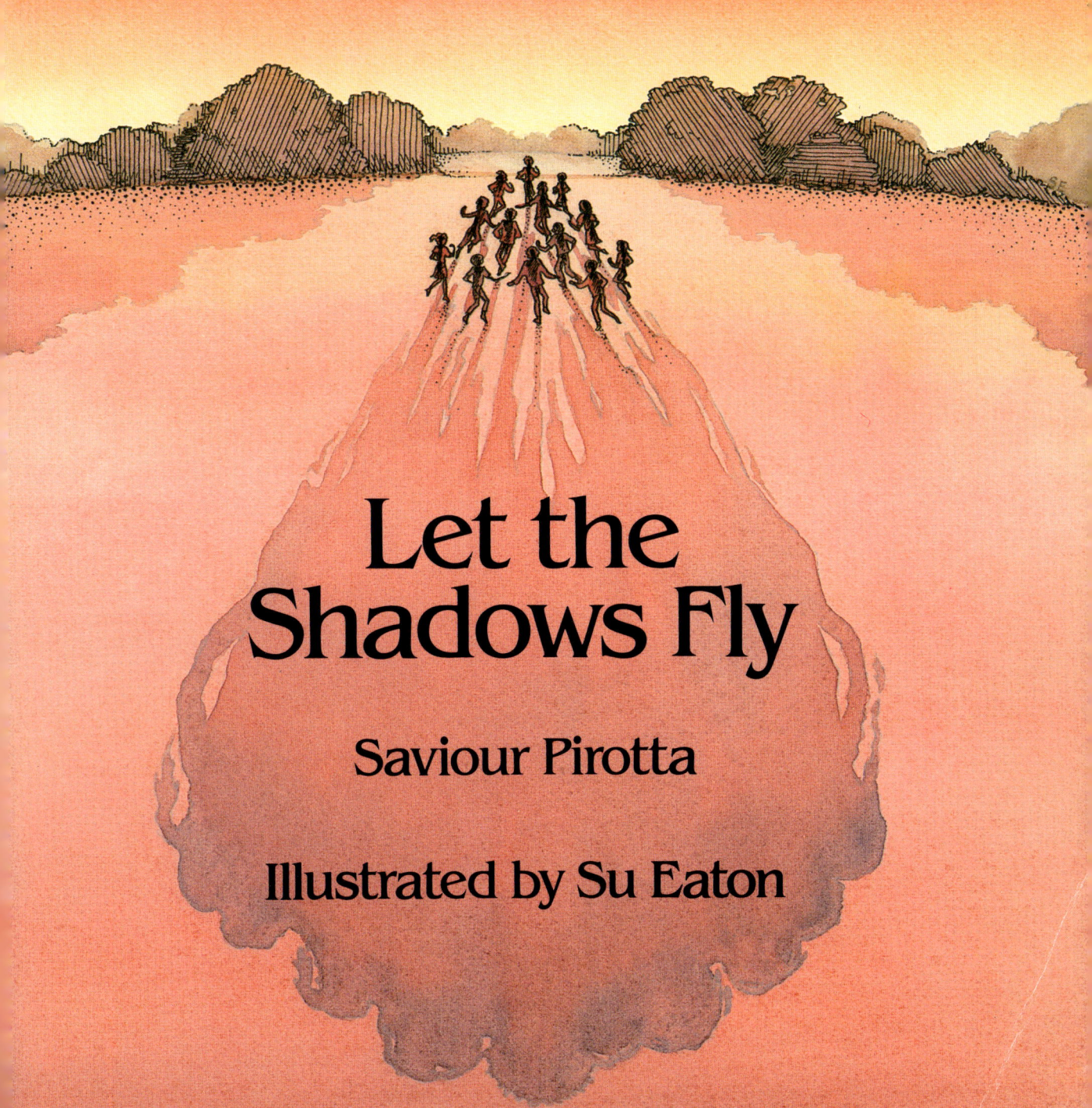

Hamish Hamilton · London

A strange new boy arrived on the Common one evening and said, 'Hey, let's build a magic castle.'

A dozen heads peeped out of their hiding places in the trees and nodded. 'Let's build a magic castle.'

'Over here,' said the strange new boy, drawing a circle with a piece of purple chalk. 'Where the shadow of the poplar meets the shadow of the elm.'

Twenty four eager hands helped build a magnificent castle with walls of ancient cardboard. On the front door they hung up a sign that said FRAGILE. Above the back door they hung HANDLE WITH CARE.

For windows they used discarded picture frames with forgotten relatives smiling through dusty panes. For turrets they added battered old soup cans and biscuit tins with fading letters.

When the castle was ready, the strange new boy ordered everyone inside and said, 'Let us close the gate.'
And the gate was closed.

The night inside the castle was much darker than the night outside.
'Let us dig,' said the strange new boy.

One hundred and twenty fingers started to dig. They scraped and scooped and scratched.

When a hundred and twenty fingernails were as dark as the night around them, they came upon something hard and smooth lying in the earth.

Twelve right hand knuckles rapped on one hard surface.
'It's a tea-chest,' muttered one mouth.
'A coffin,' said two lips.
'A blackboard.'
'A brick.'
'Ssshhh,' whispered the strange new boy. 'Haul the treasure chest up.'

Twenty four hands lifted the chest out of its grave. Twelve grubby handkerchiefs wiped it clean.

'Let us see the light,' said the strange new boy, and the chest started to shine like a million glow worms on a vine. 'Now,' said the boy. 'Open the chest.'

Fumbling hands turned rusted keys and unfastened tiny padlocks. Inside the chest lay four Egyptian candles: one red, one green, one blue and one yellow.

'Light the candles,' the strange new boy said. 'And let the shadows fly.'

They lit the first candle and . . .

suddenly their shadows on the wall were a roaring tiger with fire in its tail and embers in its eyes.

'Let the shadows fly,' whispered the strange new boy.

They opened a window for the tiger to jump through and suddenly a dozen mothers in a dozen houses thought they saw the shadow of a large cat leap through the kitchen window and gobble up all the vegetables for dinner.

They lit the second candle and . . .

suddenly their shadows on the wall were a flying vulture with green emeralds in its eyes and green fire in its claws.

'Let the shadows fly,' said the strange new boy.

They removed a tile from the ceiling and the vulture flew up and away to where a dozen fathers fancied they saw the ghost of a large bird cross their television screens and enter the cupboard where the slippers were kept.

They lit the third candle and . . .

suddenly their shadows on the wall were a great rhinoceros with blue ashes on its back and blue crystal in its horn.

'Let the shadows fly,' said the strange new boy.

They took down a wall and the rhino tore out and down the hill where a dozen mothers thought they heard a mighty rumpus going on upstairs as if something huge was drinking up all the water in the bath.

They lit the fourth candle and . . .

suddenly their shadows on the wall were coiling into a long and dangerous serpent with golden eyes and a golden tongue.

'Let the shadows fly,' said the strange new boy.

They took a lid off a turret through which the serpent slid and was gone to visit a dozen fathers who thought they saw the shadow of a large snake creep up the stairs and into the bedroom where the children's homework lay.

Then they heard a policeman's whistle and suddenly the night inside the castle was much lighter than the night outside.

'Now,' said the strange new boy. 'Let us go home.' And all the children burst out of the castle and ran home across the Common.

And presently it was discovered that there were no vegetables to eat for dinner, no slippers to fetch for father, no water to bathe in, and no homework to do.

So a dozen children were sent to bed quite early.

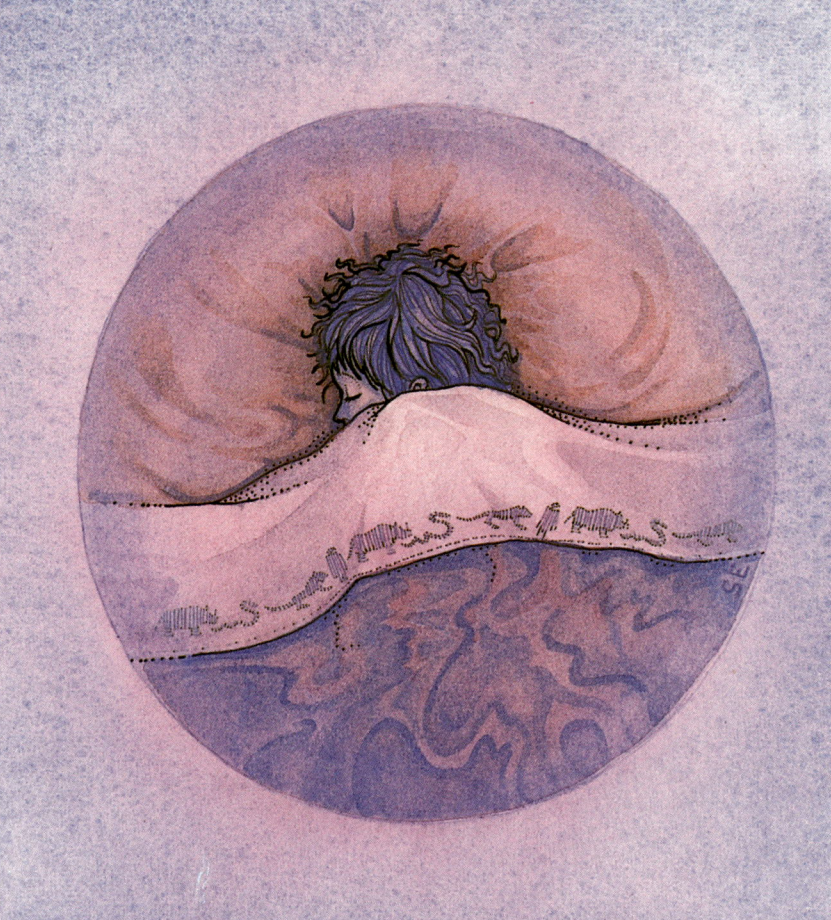

And they all slept well.